FAR LEFT Engraving of the Earl's Palace and Cathedral (1802) by J. Spottiswood
LEFT G...oyle on the ... of the ...
...**TRE** ... detail

Introduction

Towering above the Kirkwall landscape, St Magnus Cathedral, with its distinctive sandstone hues, is one of Orkney's most magnificent landmarks. Parts of this impressive building have stood for more than 850 years and its attractive appearance owes much to the polychromatic effect of the alternating stonework, comprising red sandstone quarried from Head of Holland, north of Kirkwall, and yellow sandstone which is believed to have been quarried on Eday, one of Orkney's Northern Isles.

Sandstone is extremely soft and the weathering effects of Orcadian wind and rain over the course of time have helped create pleasing, almost sculptured effects that add to the Cathedral's charm. Sir Henry Dryden considered the stonework to be the 'finest example in Great Britain of the use of stones in two different colours' and few visitors today would disagree.

Much of the original external stonework was fashioned by medieval master masons who, it is generally believed, were trained at Durham Cathedral. Although erosion has taken its toll, good examples of the original work can still be seen in the south transept doorway and around the three doorways in the west end.

Today, St Magnus Cathedral is an active place of worship, with Church of Scotland services held every Sunday, together with other services such as weddings, funerals, school services and carol services. It is also used for concerts and other events and is run on behalf of the Orcadian people by the Orkney Islands Council. However, many visitors come simply to admire and enjoy the peace and tranquillity of a beautiful building that has been dedicated to the service of God for more than eight centuries.

RIGHT *The Cardinal* by Stanley Cursiter, RSA, PRSW, one of a series of paintings displayed in the Supper Room of Kirkwall Town Hall
FAR RIGHT *View of Kirkwall from the Peerie Sea* by Stanley Cursiter RSA, PRSW

The Story of St Magnus

St Magnus, to whom the Cathedral is dedicated, is Orkney's patron saint. His story, recorded in *Orkneyinga Saga*, begins in 1098 at a time when the Orkney earldom was divided between two brothers, the Earls Paul and Erlend. Magnus was the eldest son of Earl Erlend, while Haakon was the son of Earl Paul. Unfortunately the two cousins, Haakon and Magnus, rarely agreed, and the differences between them widened as time went on.

Magnus was said to be the more popular of the two leaders, a pious man of peace and great authority, while Haakon was known to be warlike and envious of the popularity of his cousin. Discord between the cousins reached a head around 1117 when followers of the two earls arranged to bring them together at a reconciliatory Easter meeting on the island of Egilsay, about 12 km north of Kirkwall. Both earls agreed to bring two ships and a limited number of men, but Earl Haakon broke the agreement and arrived with eight ships full of armed men.

Earl Magnus crossed to the island despite an ominous great wave appearing out of the sea and crashing down on the stern of his ship, and he spent the time waiting for his cousin's arrival in prayer. When Earl Haakon arrived, Magnus refused to allow his men to defend him against his cousin and tried to settle matters in an amicable way, praying to God for assistance. He then made three offers to Haakon in an attempt to relieve his cousin of the guilt of killing him: he would go on a pilgrimage to Rome or Jerusalem and never return to Orkney; he would be imprisoned for the rest of his life; or he would be blinded, maimed and cast into a dungeon. Haakon was willing to accept the last offer but his powerful advisers insisted that Magnus must die.

The unhappy task fell to Haakon's cook, Lifolf,

The murals pictured on these pages were made by pupils from the Isle of Arran and were presented in 1980 to the people of Orkney

BELOW The box in which the bones of St Magnus were discovered in 1919 (The Orkney Museum)
RIGHT The bones of St Magnus

who took up an axe and killed Magnus. Magnus's last words were 'Take heart, poor fellow, and don't be afraid. I've prayed to God to grant you his mercy'.

Magnus was initially buried in Christ's Church, Birsay, and soon there were stories of miraculous cures associated with his burial place. Bowing to growing public opinion, the Bishop of Orkney declared Magnus a saint, and the day of his death, 16 April, was chosen as the day of his martyrdom. St Magnus's fame spread far and wide and churches were dedicated to his name in places as far afield as Faroe, Iceland and London, whilst hymns dedicated to him have survived in both Gaelic and Latin. Following the death of Magnus, Earl Haakon made pilgrimages to Rome and Jerusalem and, during the remaining years of his rule of the islands, he became a peaceful and popular earl.

In 1129, Magnus's nephew came from Norway, overthrew Haakon's son, Paul, and became Earl of Orkney. He had been born Kali Kolson but when he came to Orkney he took the name of Rognvald in memory of a previous earl of that name. He made a vow that if he succeeded in regaining the earldom, he would have a church of stone built at Kirkwall in Orkney 'so that there be not any more magnificent in the land; and let it be dedicated to Saint Magnus and to it may be brought his relics and with them the Episcopal seat'.

Thus St Magnus Cathedral was founded primarily as a final resting place for the relics of St Magnus. Work on its construction started in 1137. Rognvald was buried in the great Church he had founded and, 30 years after his death, the Bishop of Orkney also had his relics enshrined there. To this day, the remains of both St Magnus and St Rognvald lie within the Cathedral.

RIGHT Statue of St Magnus from the 14th century (The Orkney Museum) and the burial place of St Magnus, south of the organ screen
CENTRE RIGHT The plaque marking the burial place of St Magnus, south of the organ screen

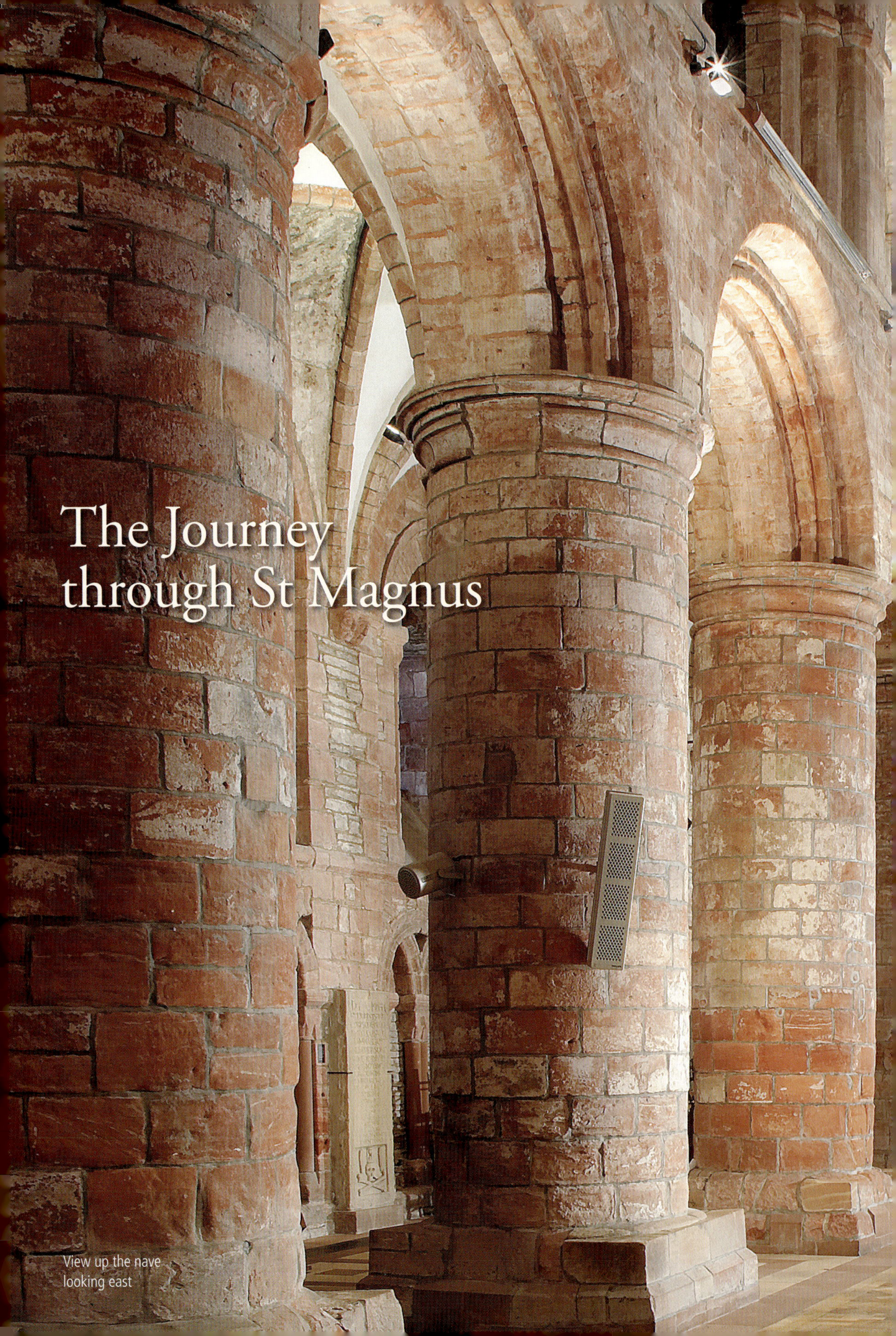

The Journey through St Magnus

View up the nave looking east

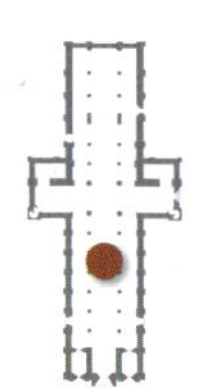

BELOW A shaft of light from the west window
LEFT The arches of the nave and triforium
BELOW LEFT The 19th-century font, dedicated to the memory of Rev. James Stuart (1834–1883). Carved around its rim are Bible extracts from *Mark 10:14* and *Luke 18:16*
FACING PAGE Looking west down the nave

Nave

The nave of the Cathedral is particularly impressive. Along part of its length it has a series of blind Romanesque-style arches which were constructed both for ornamental purposes and to decrease the weight of the walls. Note the magnificently carved five-metre-high screen for the west main door, whch was designed by George Mackie Watson and installed in the early 20th century. The bold stained glass west window, paid for by public subscription, was created by Crear McCartney to mark the occasion of the 850th anniversary and was unveiled by Queen Elizabeth II in August 1987.

FAR LEFT Stained glass windows in the south nave aisle
LEFT Gravestone of Elizabeth Cuthbert, who died in 1685. Her husband James Wallace was Minister of the Cathedral
BELOW Stained glass window depicting St Augustine

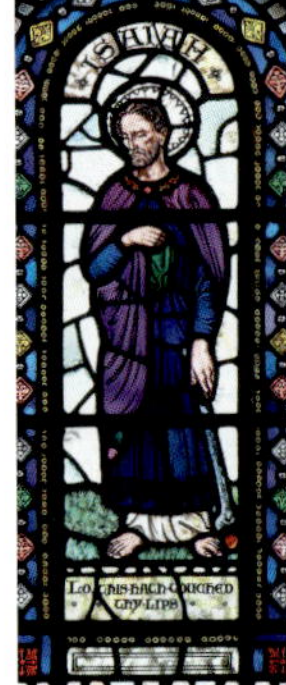

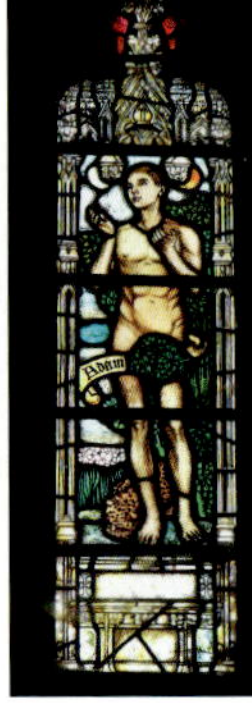

South Nave Aisle

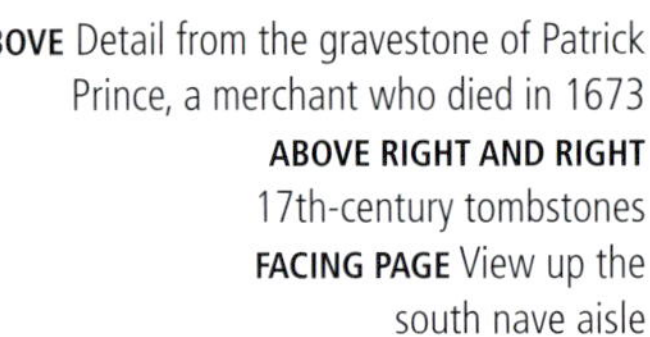

ABOVE Detail from the gravestone of Patrick Prince, a merchant who died in 1673
ABOVE RIGHT AND RIGHT 17th-century tombstones
FACING PAGE View up the south nave aisle

The majority of the tombstones standing against the inside walls of the nave aisles date from the 17th century. Originally these tombstones were on the floor of the nave. However, an arched recess in the south wall is believed to date back to the 14th century and has been identified from its coat of arms as the tomb of a native Orkney family, the Paplays.

AUG: 1750
HERE·WAS·INTERRD·THE
CORPS·OF·MARY·YOUNG
SPOUSE·TO·JOHN·RIDDOCH
THEN·ONE·OF·THE·MAGI
STRATES·OF·KIRKWALL
&AFTERWARDS·PROVOST
OF·SAID·BURGH

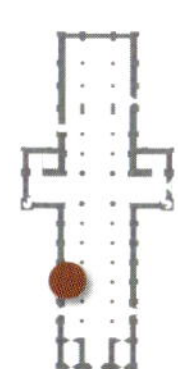

FACING PAGE Elaborate 'blind' wall arcading
TOP Douglas Strachan stained glass
ABOVE A surviving fragment of medieval floral decoration
BELOW An interesting example of a 17th-century gravestone

North Nave Aisle

ABOVE AND RIGHT The 17th-century Mort Brod memorial to Robert Nicholson, a glazier, whose son James almost certainly painted both this and the face of the Cathedral clock and its two sundials

Blind arcading is evident in the north nave aisle up to its fifth bay; the bay which probably marks the end of the Cathedral's first building campaign. A curious memorial known as the Mort Brod (meaning *death board*), in the form of a wooden hatchment with a rhyming inscription painted on one side and a shrouded skeleton on the other, hangs from one of the mighty pillars. Nearby there is evidence of the red and black paintwork which once adorned the plaster.

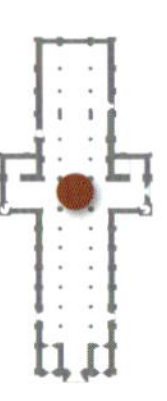

LEFT An iron ring, probably from around 1651, which was used by Cromwell's troops to tether horses

ABOVE The fine 19th-century rose window restored in 2004
RIGHT Mercat cross in the north transept
FAR RIGHT The south transept

Crossing and Transepts

FAR LEFT The pulpit and north transept
LEFT Original mason's mark in the crossing

The crossing, choir, transepts and around two-thirds of the nave were completed by the 1150s and, consequently, some of the Cathedral's oldest masonry can be seen in these areas. Extensive rebuilding of the crossing was required after its collapse circa 1170–80, however, and new square chapels, possibly based on similar rectangular chapels at Nidaros (Trondheim) Cathedral, were also built in the transepts at this time. In these chapels the narrow pointed windows are in the early Gothic style.

LEFT The St Magnus window in the north transept, designed by Oscar Patterson in the 1920s, depicts St Magnus carrying a martyr's palm and large sword
BELOW Detail of pulpit

ABOVE Knights templar cross in the south transept
RIGHT Silver chalice gifted by Rev. J. Wallace, Kirkwall, 1688
FAR RIGHT The Norwegian Bible gifted by the people of Hordaland. The oak communion table inlaid with an interlocking Celtic design was crafted by Colin William Kerr in 1991

St Magnus Cathedral has the distinction of being the only cathedral in the British Isles with its own dungeon: Marwick's Hole. Located between the south wall of the choir and the south transept chapel, it is known to have held men and women imprisoned as late as the 18th century.

Against a wall of the north transept stands Kirkwall's Market Cross which is dated 1621 and which has been brought into the Cathedral for preservation.

Choir

Fine carvings decorate the impressive organ screen and pew-ends

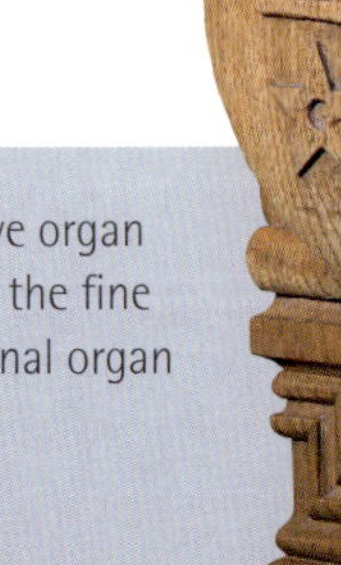

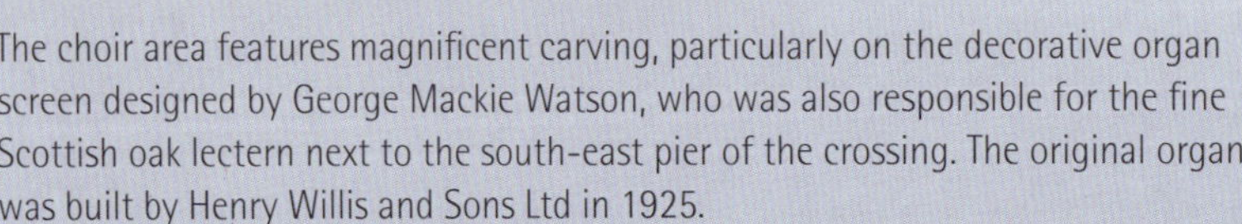

The choir area features magnificent carving, particularly on the decorative organ screen designed by George Mackie Watson, who was also responsible for the fine Scottish oak lectern next to the south-east pier of the crossing. The original organ was built by Henry Willis and Sons Ltd in 1925.

During major restoration work in 1919 some of the ashlar stones on the rectangular pier of the choir's south arcade were found to be loose. Within a cavity behind these stones the relics of St Magnus were found in a casket (pictured page 3) which is now in The Orkney Museum in Tankerness House. The relics themselves were restored to their resting place in the choir.

ABOVE Stone carved head in the south choir aisle

LEFT A tapestry in the south choir aisle was given in August 1987 to the people of Orkney by Hordaland Council, Norway, to mark the 850th anniversary of the founding of the Cathedral. It was presented by King Olaf V of Norway to Queen Elizabeth the Queen Mother, then patron of The Friends of St Magnus Cathedral

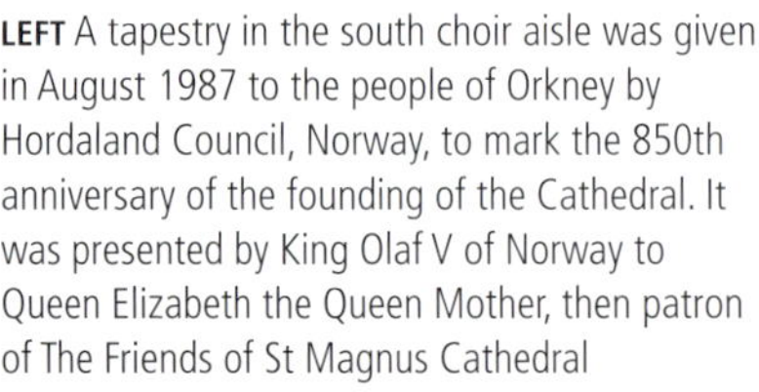

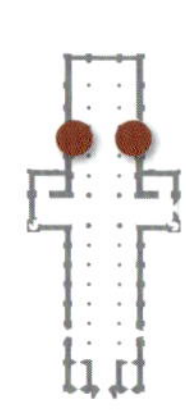

The Choir Aisles

ABOVE The Cathedral's oldest surviving tombstone, dating from the 13th century
LEFT Memorial to the 833 men of HMS *Royal Oak* drowned in Scapa Flow in October 1939, after being torpedoed by a German U-boat. The ship's bell was recovered from the wreck
FACING PAGE View up the north choir aisle

Two ornately carved arched oak screens divide the choir aisles of the Cathedral and the crossing. Designed by George Mackie Watson, they were carved by Scott Morton and Company. The tomb of Bishop Thomas Tulloch stood in this part of the Cathedral until the 17th century when Cromwell's troops destroyed most of it while they were garrisoned there. The remains of Bishop Tulloch's tomb can now be seen in The Orkney Museum.

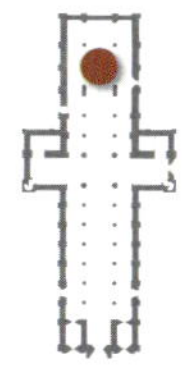

The furniture including the prayer desk (**RIGHT**) and the figures of Kol (**BOTTOM**) St Rognvald (**LEFT**) and Bishop William the Old (**BELOW LEFT**) were designed by a native of Kirkwall, Dr Stanley Cursiter, the Queen's Limner and Painter in Scotland, and made by local craftsman, Reynold Eunson

BELOW The 17th-century wooden panels which are now incorporated into the new communion table

St Rognvald Chapel

FACING PAGE St Rognvald Chapel

FAR RIGHT Two depictions of the Green Man. Originally a fertility symbol, it was used by the medieval Church to represent corruption of the flesh, the leaves representing decay and sin

In 1965, the east end of the choir (part of which dates from the 13th century) was designated St Rognvald Chapel. New furnishings were dedicated in the chapel in 1966 and these incorporated 16th- and 17th-century carved panels which had previously been preserved in the Cathedral.

Haakon Haakonsson was one of the greatest of the Norwegian Kings. In December 1263 he died in the Bishop's Palace on his way home from the Battle of Largs. In the floor a marble plaque donated by the Norwegian Government commemorates his temporary burial in the Cathedral.

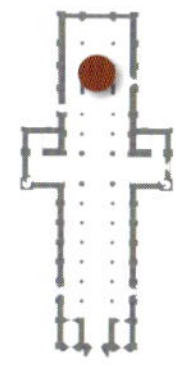

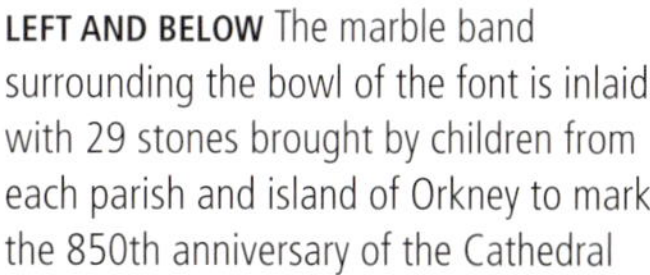

LEFT AND BELOW The marble band surrounding the bowl of the font is inlaid with 29 stones brought by children from each parish and island of Orkney to mark the 850th anniversary of the Cathedral

FACING PAGE Statue of St Olaf presented by the Bishop of Nidaros as a gift from the Church of Norway on the occasion of the Cathedral's 800th anniversary

LEFT The monument to John Rae, an Orcadian Arctic explorer and intrepid discoverer of the fate of Sir John Franklin's last expedition

BELOW The floor tiles were taken from an earlier design and were manufactured by Craven Dunnil

RIGHT Plaques commemorating Orcadians eminent in the arts

St Rognvald Chapel

LEFT Monument to William Balfour Baikie, an Orcadian explorer who travelled extensively in Africa

BELOW RIGHT Dragons on the north side of the east window

French influence has been detected in the chapel's pillars and sharp-eyed visitors may spot small human figures and animal forms among the decoration.

ABOVE 17th-century Dutch collection plate
RIGHT A leaf window, the pattern of which was once prevalent in the Cathedral
BELOW The Cathedral and tower from the south-west
FACING PAGE Looking along the south nave triforium
FACING PAGE BOTTOM Clock made by Hugh Gordon of Aberdeen in 1761 (**LEFT**) which was replaced in the early 20th century; the present clock mechanism (**RIGHT**)

Triforium Gallery and Tower

The Cathedral houses many treasures for visitors to discover. The tower was built in the 14th century and the south triforium of the nave contains the remains of a pulpit dated 1689, which was made by William Tait at an original cost of £50 Scots. In the South Triforium Gallery there is an interesting display of four stained glass windows from the early 20th-century restoration of the Cathedral. The Cathedral bells date from 1528. The largest was recast in 1682 after the tower was struck by lightning and the bells dropped onto earth placed in the crossing in an attempt to cushion their fall.

Hugh Gordon
ABERDEEN
1761

MAKERS

FAR LEFT Reverend J. Wallace's Orkney Autograph (1684) now in Orkney Library and Archive
LEFT Daniell engraving of the Cathedral and palace from the south-east

History and Restoration

The Cathedral has seen numerous alterations and modifications during the course of its long history and the wonderful building which greets visitors today is an amalgamation of the work of countless craftsmen from many different eras.

As described earlier in this guidebook, the Cathedral's founder was Earl Rognvald who supervised the earliest stages of the building in 1137 during the bishopric of William the Old of Orkney (1102–68). Bishop William was probably responsible for initiating the building of the bishop's residence in Kirkwall, now known as The Bishop's Palace.

The original St Magnus Cathedral was closely modelled on Durham Cathedral and although only fragments survive today, the walls, ceilings and pillars would have originally been plastered and painted with colourful floral patterns.

ABOVE Musket ball indentations
ABOVE RIGHT The Earl's Palace
BACKGROUND Drawing of the Cathedral by Sir Henry Dryden (1845)

By 1152 the choir and three pillars of the nave had been built and a temporary west front had been erected. The foundations for twin towers on the west front were discovered by workmen in the early 20th century, but it seems these were never built.

By the mid-12th century the apse was also in existence at the east end of the Cathedral, behind the high altar. Many centuries later the casket containing the bones of St Magnus was discovered in this area.

Between 1154 and 1472, Orkney was ecclesiastically under the Norwegian archbishop of Nidaros (Trondheim) and, after that, it became part of the Scottish province of St Andrews. The Cathedral was assigned to the inhabitants of Kirkwall by King James III of Scotland in a charter dated 1486. One of the most notable bishops was Bishop Robert Reid who held the see of Orkney between 1541 and 1558. An adviser of King James V and a very successful statesman, he was responsible for rebuilding the Bishop's Palace in Kirkwall, adding the imposing round tower which still stands today. When he died, he bequeathed a sum of money to found a college in Edinburgh and this later became Edinburgh University.

TOP LEFT Exterior view of the rose window
TOP RIGHT Daniell engraving of the Cathedral from the north-west

In 1560 the Church of Scotland was reformed and the first Reformed Minister of Kirkwall was Gilbert Foulzie, who lived in part of the building now known as Tankerness House, opposite the Cathedral. Reverend Foulzie was responsible for the arched gateway to the House's paved courtyard and his initials are carved there. The Reformation brought ruin to many cathedrals, but St Magnus Cathedral seems to have emerged relatively unscathed, although the organ, treasures and rich vestments were removed and the wall decorations were covered in whitewash. Services were held in the choir where important families were allowed to set up their own pews. It is also recorded that the Cathedral originally had a lofty spire made of wood but that this was struck by lightning in 1671, causing a fire to break out and the bells to fall to the ground.

Illustrations
of
SOME PARTS
of the
Cathedral-Church
Dedicated to
S. Magnus.
at
KIRKWALL in ORKNEY,
Architectural Institute of Scotland
1868–1871

In 1845, the Government presumed the ownership of the Cathedral, expelling the then congregation and carrying out major restoration work to the fabric of the building. It was around this time that the bones of Bishop William the Old and Bishop Thomas Tulloch were discovered. Then, in 1851, the Royal Burgh of Kirkwall re-established ownership of the building and the choir and presbytery were fitted with new pews and galleries for the reinstated congregation.

Sir Henry Dryden carried out detailed studies of the building in the mid-19th century and many of his original drawings still survive (see left), but the Cathedral slowly deteriorated until the early 20th century when the Thoms Bequest made further major restoration possible. George Hunter Thoms was Sheriff of Orkney, Caithness and Zetland from 1870–99 and, when he died, he left around £60,000 to the Cathedral for its restoration. Three architects

TOP LEFT The Cathedral from the south
TOP RIGHT The Bishop's Palace

submitted competitive restoration plans and the Council decided to proceed with the scheme submitted by George Mackie Watson of Edinburgh.

Between 1913 and 1930, the main alteration to the exterior of the Cathedral was the erection of a tall steeple which replaced the low pyramid roof of the bell tower. Internally, the screen separating the choir from the nave was removed, along with the pews and galleries. Stained glass windows replaced the formerly plain windows, much of the floor was tiled and the warm red sandstone was revealed by the removal of plaster and whitewash.

However, by the 1960s it had become evident that the building was in serious danger of subsiding. Sinking foundations meant that the nave was gradually leaning westward and the gable was in danger of collapsing into Broad Street. An Appeal Committee raised £300,000 and, by 1974, steel support girders were in place, concealed above the nave and clerestory. A Service of Thanksgiving was held in 1974 in the presence of Queen Elizabeth the Queen Mother, to mark the saving of the Cathedral.

Following reorganisation of local government in 1975 responsibility passed to the new Orkney Islands Council.

Further work has been carried out since that time and the maintenance of the Cathedral has been assigned to skilled masons who ensure that, wherever possible, the original stonework is retained. Thanks to their skill and the devotion of countless others who look after this magnificent building on a day-to-day basis, St Magnus Cathedral remains a lasting testament to the glory of God.

TOP RIGHT *The nave under restoration* by Stanley Cursiter RSA, PRSW, 1914
TOP LEFT *The Lammas Fair*, also by Stanley Cursiter. The Fair was held each August
FAR LEFT The Cathedral from the north-west
LEFT One of the west doorways showing the erosion of the stones

St Magnus Centre

The award-winning St Magnus Centre consists of a refurbished hall and an extension that provides modern facilities for young and old.

The Centre maintains the historic link between the Cathedral and the arts by providing space and encouragement for local musicians, writers and dramatists. Its spaces can also be used for small-scale exhibitions and events such as the St Magnus Festival and the Orkney Science Festival.

A highlight of any visit to the St Magnus Centre is the multi-lingual audio-visual presentation of the 'Saga of St Magnus'. The video presentation, which was financed by The Society of the Friends of St Magnus Cathedral, features narration by the renowned broadcaster, Tom Fleming and text by former Minister of the Cathedral, Reverend Ron Ferguson.

The study library, which features beautiful Norwegian timber and slate, was a gift from Norway. It incorporates the image of the ancient St Magnus Pilgrim's Cross from the contemporary Cathedral west window. Equipped with resources for young people and adults, it also has a section of books about Orkney and Norway.

To appreciate fully the history and the beauty of the Cathedral, it is strongly recommended that visitors view the video presentation before their visit to the Cathedral itself.

TOP LEFT The interior of the St Magnus Centre
TOP RIGHT The exterior of the St Magnus Centre
RIGHT The beautiful stained glass by Crear McCartney in the library of the St Magnus Centre
FAR RIGHT Sunday worship in the Cathedral
BELOW The Cathedral choir